You read two  was justified. Ir we are justified he says (so clearly, ... you remember his exact words): "You see that a person is justified by works and not by faith alone." Now you have two problems. Problem 1: there seems to be a contradiction. Problem 2: Pastor Paul is in fact *Paul the apostle*, and Pastor James is *James the brother of our Lord*. What are you supposed to do? In *Root and Fruit* two of the most influential preachers of our time patiently explain the Scriptures and help us to resolve the "problem." Spoiler alert from John Calvin: If you think you can receive Christ for justification without receiving him for sanctification, you "rend Christ asunder."

—Sinclair B Ferguson,
Teaching Fellow, Ligonier Ministries

Compare James 2:24 with Romans 3:28 as isolated verses and you might assume Paul and James were disagreeing. But pay attention to context, and a totally different understanding emerges. James is refuting libertines; Paul is repudiating legalism. They were standing together in defense of justification by faith, fighting different enemies who were attacking the gospel from opposite sides. Joel Beeke and Steve Lawson unpack and analyze these texts with great care and extraordinary clarity, proving definitively that Paul and James were in full agreement on every point of gospel truth. This is a supremely helpful book on a tough subject—more valuable than most volumes weighing in at twenty times the page count.

—John MacArthur
Pastor-Teacher, Grace Community Church

This work is clear, concise, and straight to the heart of the matter. It confirms the harmony of Scripture and demonstrates how Paul and James provide us with a complete and unified picture of the doctrine of justification without the smallest measure of contradiction. The proverb that "an ounce of prevention is worth a pound of cure" surely applies here. The truths in this brief work will put many new converts on the right path and aid pastors in counseling the souls that have been entrusted to them. It would be extremely useful in evangelism, counseling, and small group book studies.

—Paul David Washer,
Director, HeartCry Missionary Society

We owe a great debt to Joel Beeke and Steven Lawson for this book. It helps us see that there is no contradiction between James and Paul in their understanding and teaching of justification. A right doctrinal understanding of the gospel is crucial for salvation and for a buoyant sense of assurance of salvation. Therefore, we must never allow ourselves to get confused about the gospel. Our eternal salvation is by grace alone through faith alone in Jesus Christ. Yet it's a salvation that produces good works. Read this book and you will never be unsettled about this matter again!

—Conrad Mbewe,
Pastor, Kabwata Baptist Church

ROOT
&
FRUIT

Harmonizing Paul and
James on Justification

ROOT & FRUIT

Harmonizing Paul and James on Justification

JOEL R. BEEKE &
STEVEN J. LAWSON

FREE GRACE PRESS

Root and Fruit

Harmonizing Paul and James on Justification

Copyright © 2020 by Joel R. Beeke and Steven J. Lawson

All rights reserved. Written permission must be secured from the author to use or reproduce any part of this book, except for brief quotations in critical reviews or articles.

Free Grace Press
1076 Harkrider
Conway, AR 72032
freegracepress.com

Cover design by Dustin Benge

Unless otherwise noted, all Scripture references in this book are taken from the King James Version, public domain.

Scripture marked (NKJV) taken from the New King James Version®. Copyright © 1982 by Thomas Nelson. Used by permission. All rights reserved.

ISBN: 978-1-952599-01-9

This book is an expanded and collated version of addresses the authors gave at the 2010 Philadelphia Conference on Reformed Theology (PCRT).

Contents

	Introduction	11
1.	The Root of Justification	21
2.	The Means of Justification	29
3.	Saving Faith	37
4.	The Fruit of Justification	45
5.	Non-Saving Faith	51
6.	Justified by Faith or by Works	55
7.	The Root Produces the Fruit	65

Introduction

We must be right about the doctrine of justification for several important reasons. First, this doctrine not only lies at the heart of the gospel, it *is* the gospel. Second, justification is the greatest antidote to heresy. Nearly all heresies have stemmed from a misunderstanding of this doctrine. Third, justification is a great incentive to a revived church. Only God can send revival, but true revival is never without a rediscovery of such basic biblical truth as justification by faith alone. Fourth, justification greatly impacts a vast array of pastoral problems, such as the lack of assurance of faith and an inability to handle trials Christianly. Fifth, the whole of the Christian life is little more than an ongoing discovery of the glory and power of justification. The tragedy of our Christian lives and the reason there may be so little power in our ongoing sanctification is because we have ceased to wonder at our justification.

It is one thing, however, to acknowledge that it is crucial to be right about justification for many weighty reasons, but it is another to practically and pastorally answer the question *Who is justified?*

Assume for a moment that you are a pastor and your church requires for membership a verbal testimony of a credible profession of faith before the pastors and elders. Let me introduce you to two men, Mr. Jones and Mr. Smith, two typical test cases, who are applying for membership in your church and desire to partake of the Lord's Supper.

In the presence of your elders, you ask Mr. Jones, "On what basis do you believe you are a Christian and should be received into the fellowship of this church?" Mr. Jones responds, "Well, I think my entire life shows that I am a solid Christian. I have grown up in the church and have always been religious. I believe the Bible is the inerrant Word of God and have soundly Reformed, biblical beliefs. I read the Bible and pray every day and never miss a church service. I give my money to the church, and I am very generous to Christian organizations and charities. I attend as many Reformed conferences as I can. I am a faithful husband, a good father, and a loyal worker. On these grounds, I believe that I am a Christian, and I trust you will receive me into your church fellowship as a fellow believer."

Mr. Jones leaves the room, and Mr. Smith then appears before you. You're a bit concerned about what he is going to say because he has not been attending church faithfully. You ask him the same question you asked Mr. Jones, and you are pleasantly surprised. Mr. Smith answers energetically and succinctly, "My answer is simple: I've been born again. I have been justified, I'm saved, and I trust in the blood of Christ alone for salvation. All praise be to the sovereign grace of God. Hallelujah!"

You then ask Mr. Smith to leave the room a moment as you discuss these two cases. You look around at your elders. You sense on their faces that they are more impressed with Mr. Smith than with Mr. Jones. Sure enough, one elder says, "There certainly is no doubt about Mr. Smith's case. He has all the basics: He can tell us the right things about being saved, being justified, and having Christ. We can be grateful that this brother is an evangelical believer."

You sigh to yourself and then regretfully pull from your pocket a letter from Mr. Smith's previous minister. "Brothers," you say, "I am afraid that I have a letter here that I have to read to you." You then read:

> I would counsel you that if you ever interview Mr. Smith for membership, beware. He can talk like an angel, but I am warning you, he is very inconsistent

in his walk of life. At times he has verbally abused his wife, such that she has lost every shred of respect for him, and is unkind to his own children. He often does not do an honest day's work. He cannot accept any loving rebuke. On Sunday, he looks and talks like a mature believer, but his life doesn't match up to what he professes during the week.

Well then, who should you accept? Mr. Jones? Mr. Smith? Neither of them? Both?

Let us hold you at bay for a moment before we answer these questions. To get justification right and to understand it practically and pastorally so we can answer such questions correctly, we need to rightly understand the relationship of Paul and James on this critical subject. The relationship between Romans 3:21–28 and James 2:14–26 has long been a source of controversy in the church. The apostle Paul writes in unquestionable language that a man is justified by faith *alone*, apart from any works. James seems to contradict him by writing, in equally clear language, that a man is justified by faith and works.

So, which is it? Is a man justified by faith, or is he justified by faith and works? Is James in contradiction to Paul? Is Paul in controversy with James? Who is right? This dilemma over the means of justification has long puzzled many in the church.

A Gateway to Heaven

Nearly five hundred years ago, a professor of Bible at the University of Wittenberg named Martin Luther was teaching the book of Romans to his students when he became increasingly convinced that the central theme of Romans is justification by faith alone.

Luther came under deep conviction of this truth and was brought to the great crisis point of his life, when he put his faith in the person and work of Jesus Christ. Sometime between 1514 and 1519, Luther was radically converted to Christ in what is called his "Tower Experience." Luther later wrote of this dramatic experience:

> I greatly longed to understand Paul's epistle to the Romans, and nothing stood in the way but that one expression "the righteousness of God," because I took it to mean that righteousness whereby God is righteous and deals righteously in punishing the unrighteous. . . . Night and day I pondered until . . . I grasped the truth that the righteousness of God is that righteousness whereby, through grace and sheer mercy, he justifies us by faith. Thereupon I felt myself to be reborn and to have

gone through open doors into paradise. The whole of Scripture took on a new meaning. Whereas before "the righteousness of God" had filled me with hate, now it became to me inexpressibly sweet in greater love. This passage of Paul became to me a gateway to heaven.[2]

Suddenly, Luther saw and understood from the book of Romans that the justification of the sinner by God is on the basis of faith alone in Christ alone. Justification by faith alone became the very cornerstone doctrine of the Reformation in the sixteenth century, and it continues to be the anchor point for every true church today. It is, as Luther wrote, the very article on which the church stands or falls.

This is as true now as it was in the sixteenth century, when Luther fought for this doctrine, and in the first century, when Paul and James wrote. Some today, under the nomenclature of the New Perspective on Paul, essentially argue for a faith-and-works basis for salvation, maintaining that salvation is based on faith and perseverance in good works. Of course, as we shall see, true faith always issues in works, but we are not

---

[2] Quoted in F. F. Bruce, *The Letter of Paul to the Romans: An Introduction and Commentary* (Grand Rapids: Eerdmans, 1985), 57.

saved by faith plus persevering works. It is faith alone that God employs as the instrument of salvation.

A Right Strawy Epistle

A short time later Luther came to the book of James and sought to make sense of what it says about justification by faith and works. In the introduction to the first edition of his German New Testament, written in 1522, Luther made the following often-quoted remark about the book of James:

> St. Paul's epistles, especially those to Romans, Galatians, Ephesians, and St. Peter's first epistle, these are the books which show Christ and teach everything that is needful and blessed to know even though you never see or hear any other book or doctrine. Therefore, St. James' epistle is a right strawy epistle in comparison with them; for there is no gospel character to it.[3]

Luther called the letter of James "a right strawy epistle," meaning it appeared to him to be weak, of little content or substance regarding the gospel. Luther was confounded. He was not denying the inspiration of the

---

[3] Cf. *Luther's Works*, ed. Jaroslav Pelikan (St. Louis: Concordia, 1958), 35:362.

book of James or its canonicity. Rather, he was downplaying its value to the church in comparison to Romans because James, he estimated, contains little teaching about the great doctrines of the gospel of which Luther had become a staunch defender.

The main source of Luther's discomfort with James was the Roman Catholic Church and its teaching on justification by faith and works. Luther was correct that James is not a doctrinal treatise per se. Instead, it is an intensely practical book, a manual not on justification but on sanctification.

The question is, How do we harmonize Romans and James in this matter of justification? Paul clearly says it is by faith apart from works, and James asserts it is by faith and works.

It is helpful to note that the Reformers rightly identified a key interpretive principle, called the *analogy of faith*, or the *analogy of Scripture*. This hermeneutical principle says that the entire Bible speaks with one voice. That is, Scripture can never contradict itself. The whole of Scripture is one seamless tapestry of truth into which each thread of doctrine is perfectly woven, making one statement of truth. The Bible presents one plan of salvation.

So, we know that Paul and James cannot contradict themselves. They speak with one voice, yet how so? We want to look at these two passages separately then seek to harmonize them.

I

The Root of Justification

But now the righteousness of God without the law is manifested, being witnessed by the law and the prophets; Even the righteousness of God which is by faith of Jesus Christ unto all and upon all them that believe: for there is no difference: For all have sinned, and come short of the glory of God; Being justified freely by his grace through the redemption that is in Christ Jesus: Whom God hath set forth to be propitiation through faith in his blood, to declare his righteousness for the remission of sins that are past, through the forbearance of God; To declare, I say, at this time his righteousness: that he might be just, and the justifier of him which believeth in Jesus. Where is boasting then? It is excluded. By what law? of works? Nay: but by the law of faith. Therefore we conclude that a man is justified by faith without the deeds of the law.

Romans 3:21–28

First, we want to look at Romans 3 and 4 under the heading "The Root of Justification." Let us begin in Romans 3:21, paying careful attention to the prepositions. What we see is that justification is "by" grace (v. 24), "by" and "through" faith (vv. 22, 25, 28, 30), "in" Jesus Christ (vv. 24, 26), "without" the works of the law (vv. 21, 28).

This is the root of justification. Without this root there can be no justification, for we "all have sinned, and come short of the glory of God" (v. 23). Justification is *by* grace, *through* faith, *in* Christ, *without* the works of the law.

An Alien Righteousness

In Romans 3:21, Paul writes: "But now the righteousness of God without the law is manifested, being witnessed by the law and the prophets." Paul means that the righteousness that comes from God is entirely apart from the works of the law. Attempts at keeping the law of Moses cannot save. No one in the Old Testament, living under the law or the prophets, was ever saved by obeying the law. No amount of good works in keeping the law could ever bring a sinner to a place of righteousness before God.

In verse 22, Paul continues, "Even the righteousness of God which is by faith of Jesus Christ." In other words, God gives His righteousness to those who receive it by faith alone in Christ alone.

Luther called this righteousness an "alien" righteousness or a "foreign" righteousness. This means it is a righteousness from outside the person receiving it, one that comes from God and given freely to the sinner who believes in Jesus Christ. This alien righteousness does not originate within the believer; the believer does not work it out from within. Rather, it comes down from above, freely bestowed on that sinner who believes in Jesus Christ alone for salvation.

At the end of verse 22, Paul states: "Unto all and upon all them that believe: for there is no difference." Whether Jew or Gentile, this righteousness is for all who believe. The words *faith* and *believe* are from the same root in the Greek language (*pistis*, *pisteuo*), which doubly affirms that justification is by faith alone.

There is absolutely no mention of any contribution of any human works toward justification. In fact, at the beginning of verse 21, Paul emphatically says it is apart from the works of the law. Nothing could be clearer.

Why do all need to be justified by faith? In Romans 3:23–24, Paul explains: "For all have sinned and come short of the glory of God; being justified." To be *justified* is for God to declare the guilty sinner to be righteous, which grants a standing of full acceptance with Him. Justification is the forensic declaration of God, who credits His Son's perfect keeping of the law and righteousness to the sinner who believes.

Lest there be any misunderstanding, Paul adds, "Being justified freely by his grace through the redemption that is in Christ Jesus: whom God hath set forth to be a propitiation through faith in his blood" (vv. 24–25). Justification is by grace alone toward undeserving sinners. This righteousness is given as a free gift. There is absolutely nothing that a fallen, sinful human being can do to deserve it.

Justification is received exclusively through faith, a fact clearly taught in verses 22 and 25. Further, it is in Christ alone, as verses 22 and 24 maintain, and apart from the law, according to verse 21.

Master teacher that he is, Paul teaches this with both a negative denial and a positive assertion. Paul tells us how justification *is not received* as well as how it *is received*. There is no room for any misunderstanding.

Justification, Paul maintains, is not by the works of the law but by faith alone. It is from these very verses and surrounding context that the great *solas* of the Reformation were born. Justification is *sola gratia*, by grace alone; *sola fide*, by faith alone; *solus Christus*, in

Christ alone. This is the very essence of the gospel. And in verses 25–26 Paul says, "To declare his righteousness for the remission of sins that are past, through the forbearance of God; to declare, I say, at this time his righteousness: that he might be just, and the justifier of him which believeth in Jesus." The apostle states that the death of Christ is the sole ground of justification and faith is its exclusive means. It could not be any more lucid than this: Justification is by faith alone in Christ alone.

The Contrast between Works and Faith

Beginning in verse 27 of Romans 3, Paul now belabors the contrast between works and faith lest there be any misunderstanding. He sets it forth as an either/or situation, never as a both/and proposition. Faith and works are mutually exclusive, never inclusive, as they relate to the means of justification.

In verse 27, Paul asks, "Where is boasting then?" His whole argument is that if justification is by works, we should boast in ourselves. But if justification is by faith alone, then there is no self-boasting: "Where is boasting then? It is excluded." When Paul says this, he is referring to boasting in ourselves, as if our works could achieve justification. The apostle continues: "By what law? of works? Nay: but by the law of faith" (v. 27). He is saying that God does not justify on the basis—meaning the premise, principle, or law—of works. Instead, it is by a law of faith. In fact, it is by a law of faith *alone*.

Verse 28 is emphatic and dogmatic: "Therefore we conclude that a man is justified by faith without the deeds of the law." When Luther translated this verse from Erasmus's Greek New Testament into the German language, a work he began while hiding in the Wartburg Castle, he added the word *alone*. Although it is not found in the original text, the Reformer did this so that there would be no misunderstanding among the German people as to the means of justification. The translation, though interpretive, is justifiable in view of the only alternative—namely, justification by works—which Paul expressly repudiated.

In verses 29 and 30, Paul asks, "Is he the God of Jews only? is he not also of the Gentiles? Yes, of the Gentiles also: seeing it is one God, which shall justify the circumcision by faith, and uncircumcision through faith." Paul is saying that there is only one way of salvation taught in the Bible. There is one way of salvation for the Jew, and it is exactly the same way for the Gentile. There is one way of salvation for those in the Old Testament, and it is exactly the same in the New Testament, whether for a Jew or for a Gentile.

There is only one way of salvation, and it is by faith alone in Christ alone. Circumcision is nothing. Uncircumcision is nothing. Faith in Christ alone is everything.

2

The Means of Justification

What shall we say then that Abraham our father, as pertaining to the flesh, hath found? For if Abraham were justified by works, he hath whereof to glory; but not before God. For what saith the scripture? Abraham believed God, and it was counted unto him for righteousness. Now to him that worketh is the reward not reckoned of grace, but of debt. But to him that worketh not, but believeth on him that justifieth the ungodly, his faith is counted for righteousness.

Romans 4:1–5

Paul carries the argument of *sola fide* forward in Romans 4 and turns to the father of the entire nation of Israel, Abraham. How was Abraham saved in the Old Testament? Was Abraham saved by works or by faith? Paul now shows that Abraham was justified by faith apart from any human works. In fact, Romans 4 illustrates the instruction of Romans 3; Paul now demonstrates what he has taught in Romans 3 from the life of Abraham (vv. 1–5) as well as from David (vv. 6–8). The apostle could not set forth any two people more highly esteemed from the Old Testament than Abraham and David. He shows that both men were saved by faith alone.

Beginning in verse 1: "What shall we say then that Abraham our father, as pertaining to the flesh, hath found?" The question deals with justification. What did Abraham discover about justification? In verse 2, Paul answers the question: "For if Abraham were justified by works, he hath whereof to glory." If Abraham could be good enough to find acceptance with God through his own works, he could brag of his own human goodness. But Paul adds at the end of verse 2, "But not before God." That is, if he were boasting in his own works, it certainly would not be before God. The reason follows in verse 3: "For what saith the scripture?"

Paul now appeals to the Old Testament, affirming that justification has always been by faith alone. As an attorney would enter evidence into the public record of the courtroom, so Paul quotes Genesis 15:6 in the latter half of verse 3: "Abraham believed God, and it was counted unto him for righteousness." This verse teaches that justification is the act by which God credits His perfect righteousness to the spiritually bankrupt account of the guilty, condemned sinner who believes in Christ. We are all spiritually bankrupt before a holy God (Rom. 3:23), and "the wages of sin is death" (Rom. 6:23). We possess no spiritual capital in our account that would merit a right standing before God. In justification God takes the very righteousness of Jesus Christ and imputes it to our account. This transaction takes place by faith. When God surveys His books in heaven and looks next to our name, He sees the perfect righteousness of Christ that has been reckoned to us on the basis of faith.

Faith *Alone*: The Sole Means of Justification

The basis for the transfer of such vast riches to our account is not simply faith but faith *alone*. In Romans 4:3, Paul tells us: "Abraham believed God and it was counted unto him for righteousness." Justification is the legal imputation of God's righteousness to Abraham's account, and it was done exclusively on the basis of saving faith. Expounding this verse, Theodore Beza comments:

> Abraham was not justified, and made the father of the faithful, by any of his own works, either preceding or following his faith in Christ, as promised to him; but merely by faith in Christ, or the merit of Christ by faith imputed to him for

righteousness. Therefore all his children become his children and are justified, not by their works, either preceding or following their faith; but by faith alone in the same Christ.[1]

Paul goes on to say in verse 4, "Now to him that worketh"—referring to all human efforts of self-righteousness in keeping the law—"is the reward not reckoned of grace, but of debt." In other words, if a person could work perfectly enough to receive the righteousness of God, it would not be a gift but wages earned. Paul concludes in verse 5, "But to him that worketh not, but believeth on him that justifieth the ungodly, his faith is counted for righteousness." So, this negative denial and positive assertion state that justification is by faith *alone*.

Justification by faith alone was the tipping point for the Reformation in the sixteenth century. It was all about the recovery of the gospel of Jesus Christ. How can sinful man be made right before a holy God? How can sinners be received by a holy God? The hinge on which all religion turns, John Calvin said, is this doctrine of justification by faith. Everything swung on this pivotal doctrine. The battleground in the

---

[1] Quoted in William S. Plumer, *The Grace of Christ: or, Sinners Saved by Unmerited Kindness* (1853; repr. Keyser, WV: Odom, 1990), 244.

Reformation was how the righteousness of God was given to the guilty sinner. Is it by faith and works, or is it by faith alone? The Roman Catholic Church maintained that it was by a complex maze of faith and works. Rome asserted that it required believing and keeping the works of the law: Justification required the sacrament of baptism, church membership, the confession of sin to a priest, the buying of indulgences, spending time in purgatory, and attending Mass. It required the entirety of all of that, and still there was not enough righteousness given to the sinner.

The Works-Righteousness of Rome

If righteousness was to be realized, Rome claimed, it required tapping into the supposed treasury of merit in heaven. There are those who have already gone to heaven, Rome insisted, who had enough extra righteousness to add to their heavenly treasury box. This surplus righteousness was available to make up what was lacking in poor, stumbling sinners like you and me. So if these other means of grace were not enough, additional righteousness could be drawn from the treasury of merit.

But even all that was not necessarily enough. Even to the sinner's last dying breath on their deathbed, the priest would rush in to administer last rites in an eleventh-hour effort to get more righteousness into the account of the guilty sinner. Few in this Roman system ever have an assurance of their own salvation because this view of righteousness is based on performing works of righteousness to meet God's perfect standard. But who can ever do enough? Nevertheless, that was the position of the Roman Catholic Church defended at the Council of Trent (1545–1563), and it has never changed to this very day.

In fact, Rome only continues to add the necessity of works to the whole foul system. They added praying to the Virgin Mary as well as praying to saints to gain access to the Lord Jesus. But there *still* is not enough righteousness available. Do you know why? Because not one drop of righteousness can be given through any of those means of justification. Isaiah 64:6 says, "All our righteousnesses are as filthy rags." That is God's estimate of human self-righteousness. The word for "filthy rags" is what was used for a woman's menstrual cycle. Our works of self-righteousness are like loathsome rags in the sight of a holy God.

What Luther found—what Martin Bucer found, what Ulrich Zwingli found, what John Calvin found, and what all the Reformers found, including John Knox, as they looked into the Word of God—is this primary truth: Justification is by faith *alone*. These men spoke of the perspicuity of the Scripture, meaning that the Bible speaks with unmistakable clarity in matters of salvation. Even a little child could pick up the Scripture, read it, and understand what it says in matters of salvation. The truth would be abundantly clear to anyone who reads the Bible in dependency on the Spirit, which is that justification is by faith alone apart from any human works. That was the cannon that was fired in the sixteenth century, the shot heard around the world, and it continues to reverberate to this very day.

3

Saving Faith

R. C. Sproul writes in *The Reformation Study Bible* the following statement regarding the importance of faith: "Faith is the means or instrument by which a person is saved. Christians are justified before God by faith." Sproul clarifies what true saving faith is: "Faith cannot be defined in subjective terms as a feeling or optimistic decision. Neither is it a passive orthodoxy. Faith is a response directed toward an object and defined by what is believed. Christian faith is trust in the eternal God and His promises secured by Jesus Christ. It is called forth by the gospel as the gospel is made understood through the gracious work of the Holy Spirit."[1]

---

[1] "Faith and Works," in *The Reformation Study Bible*, ed. R. C. Sproul (Orlando: Ligonier, 2005), 1804.

What Is Saving Faith?

When Sproul says, "Christian faith," he means *saving* faith or a *living* faith—a true faith that saves. He adds: "Christian faith is a personal act involving the mind, the heart, and the will. Just as it is directed to a personal God and not an idol or an idea."[2]

Sproul is saying that saving faith is a *personal* act directed to a *personal* God. He continues:

> It is usual to analyze faith as involving three steps: knowledge, agreement, and trust. First is knowledge or acquaintance with the content of the gospel. That is to say we must first know the truth of the gospel of Jesus Christ. It is a personal act directed towards propositional truth that speaks to us concerning a personal Savior. Then second, it is agreement or recognition that the gospel is true. So, not only must I know the truth, but secondly, I must agree that this is the truth; and there is assent and consent in my heart. There is a persuasion that this is true. Third, faith is trust, the essential step of committing the self to God. So, it must go beyond the mind and beyond the emotions. It must go all the way to affect the will, where there is a decisive decision and choice that is

---

[2] "Faith and Works," 1804.

made whereby I commit my life and surrender my life to the Lord Jesus Christ. And I place my life in His saving hands, and I trust Him and Him alone to save me from my sins and to justify me before the Father in heaven.[3]

By the work of the Holy Spirit, this trusting in Christ is the nature of saving faith, and it is the very faith that the apostle Paul requires.

Before we move to James's epistle, let's answer two questions you might have. First, perhaps you would ask, *Why should salvation that justifies us come to us only by faith?* Here are two good reasons.

First, Paul repeatedly tells us that it is by faith that we get into Christ (see Eph. 1). Faith brings us into Christ so that all Christ has done for us actually becomes ours. And as it becomes ours, we receive from God everything that God has done for us in His Son. Through faith, then, Christ comes to us clothed in the garments of justification.

Second, justification is only by faith because it is God's plan in saving us to engage us personally to Jesus Christ in such a way that our bonding ourselves to Jesus contributes nothing to our salvation. This is part of the

---

[3] "Faith and Works," 1804.

inexpressible genius of the gospel. The gospel does not bring us a salvation over our heads but into our lives. And the way it brings it into our lives without for a moment compromising grace is that the means by which we receive Christ is by definition a means that contributes nothing to Christ but receives everything from Christ. Faith is, by definition, refusing to rely on myself and relying entirely on Him.

Faith, then, is a holy command, a personal necessity, and a pressing urgency (2 Kings 17:14; John 3:36). There is only faith or damnation (Mark 16:16). Faith is indispensable. As John Flavel wrote, "The soul is the life of the body; faith is the life of the soul; Christ is the life of faith."[4]

How Saving Faith Is Experienced

Second, you may ask, *How does faith experientially appropriate Christ and His righteousness?* By the Spirit and Word of God, justifying faith is a saving grace that empties me of my own righteousness and moves me to receive, rest on, and live out of Christ and His righteousness for pardon and salvation.

---

[4] John Flavel, "The Method of Grace," in *The Whole Works of the Rev. Mr. John Flavel* (London: W. Baynes, 1820), 2:104.

Faith is an experientially convicting, soul-emptying grace that makes us conscious of the desperate situation we are in because of sin and the tragic judgment we deserve; it empties us of all our righteousness and drives us to the righteousness of Christ so that we wholeheartedly "assent to the truth of the gospel" (Westminster Larger Catechism, Q. 73).

Faith believes from the heart what the Scriptures teach about us, the holiness of God, and the saviorhood of Christ. Faith surrenders to the evangel and falls into the outstretched arms of God. It flees with all the soul's poverty to Christ's riches, with all the soul's guilt to Christ as reconciler, with all the soul's bondage to Christ as liberator. Faith confesses with Augustus Toplady:

> *Nothing in my hand I bring,*
>
> *Simply to Thy cross I cling;*
>
> *Naked, come to Thee for dress;*
>
> *Helpless, look to Thee for grace;*
>
> *Foul, I to the fountain fly;*
>
> *Wash me, Savior, or I die.*

Faith, then, enables us to lay hold of Christ and His righteousness and experience pardon and the peace that passes understanding (Phil. 4:7). As John Calvin said, "It introduces us into a participation of the righteousness of

Christ."[5] It apprehends and "closes with" Christ in a warm, believing embrace, surrendering all of self, clinging to His Word, relying on His promises. Faith reposes in the person of Christ—coming, hearing, seeing, trusting, taking, embracing, knowing, rejoicing, loving, triumphing. Faith, Luther writes, clasps Christ as a ring clasps its jewel.[6] Faith appropriates with a believing heart the perfect righteousness, satisfaction, and holiness of Christ. It weds the soul to Christ and lives out of Christ. Christ is faith's only object and only expectation. Faith commits the total person to the total person of Christ.

This precious doctrine of justification by faith alone is the heart of the evangel, the kernel of the glory of the gospel of the blessed triune God, the key to the kingdom of heaven. "Justification by faith," John Murray writes, "is the jubilee trumpet of the gospel because it proclaims the gospel to the poor and destitute whose only door of hope is to roll themselves in total helplessness upon the grace and power and

---

[5] John Calvin, *Institutes of the Christian Religion*, trans. John Allen (Philadelphia: Nicklin and Howe, 1816), 2:229 [3.11.20].

[6] *Luther's Works*, 26:132.

righteousness of the Redeemer of the lost."[7] In our decadent day there is a crying need to reestablish and defend the scriptural proclamation of this doctrine. Not only is justification by faith still, in Luther's words, "the article by which the church stands or falls," but by this doctrine each of us shall personally stand or fall before God. Justification by faith alone must be confessed and experienced by you and me. It is a matter of eternal life or eternal death—and most importantly, it is a matter of God's glory.

Dear friend, have you exercised saving faith in the Lord Jesus Christ? Do you know the truth? Are you persuaded of the truth? Have you acted on the truth? By the Spirit's grace, have you been emptied of your own righteousness and been drawn to assent wholly to the gospel? Have you truly repented of sin and believed in Christ alone for salvation; have you entrusted your life to Him and His righteousness? Have you clasped Christ as a ring clasps its jewel, and are you now living out of Him as your all-in-all?

If so, then all the righteousness of Jesus Christ has been transferred by God to your account in heaven. If

---

[7] John Murray, *Collected Writings of John Murray* (Edinburgh: Banner of Truth, 1977), 2:217.

so, God looks on you and sees the perfect righteousness of Christ Himself. It is on this basis alone that God's righteousness is given to us, and it is by faith *alone*. This is the *root* of justification.

4

The Fruit of Justification

What doth it profit, my brethren, though a man say he hath faith, and have not works? can faith save him? If a brother or sister be naked, and destitute of daily food, And one of you say unto them, Depart in peace, be ye warmed and filled; notwithstanding ye give them not those things which are needful to the body; what doth it profit? Even so faith, if it hath not works, is dead, being alone. Yea, a man may say, Thou hast faith, and I have works: shew me thy faith without thy works, and I will shew thee my faith by my works.

James 2:14–18

Let us turn now to James 2 to consider the *fruit* of justification. Wherever there is the root of saving faith, there will always be its fruit. In James 2, the half-brother of Christ argues for the necessity of fruit. Paul and James are in total agreement, although at first reading, the two appear to be contradicting each other. But their teaching is related, just as the fruits of a tree (James) are related to its roots (Paul). The roots of a tree can only be determined to be alive and healthy if the fruit is healthy. The Reformers explained the apparent contradiction this way: "Faith alone saves, but faith that is alone does not save." That is, true saving faith will always be accompanied by good works that verify the validity of that faith and prove it is real.

Saving Faith vs. Non-saving Faith

The Bible speaks of a faith that saves and a faith that does not save. It speaks of a *living* faith and a *dead* faith, of a true faith that connects us to Christ and a counterfeit faith that leaves us separated from Christ. James addresses the difference between true faith and a false faith, between a saving faith and non-saving faith. People often ask, "How can I know if my faith is real?" That is what James is addressing here and throughout his epistle. In fact, the whole of James's letter is concerned with "pure and undefiled religion" (James 1:27 NKJV).

Beginning in chapter 2, verse 14, James introduces the subject of true saving faith. He asks, "What doth it profit, my brethren, though a man say he hath faith, and have not works? can faith save him?" James is acknowledging how easy it is merely to say you have faith. The word that leaps off the page is *says*—someone says. How easy it is to say, "Lord, Lord." How easy it is to give a confession of faith. How effortless it is just to verbalize, "Oh, yes, I have faith in the Lord." James is addressing the one who simply says he has faith and yet has no good works in his life. Can that faith save him? Is that real faith? Is faith without works a living faith? Does faith without works rightly connect me to the Savior and His righteousness? That is the question James raises. Could there be a more crucial issue to be raised?

Empty Words, Dead Faith

In verses 15–16, James gives an example: "If a brother or sister be naked, and destitute of daily food, and one of you say unto them"—please note, the emphasis again is on *says*—"depart in peace, be ye warmed and filled; notwithstanding ye give them not those things which are needful to the body; what doth it profit?" This is understood as a half-hearted, apathetic "depart in peace, be ye warmed and filled." These are empty words arising from a dead faith, one that has no good Samaritan-type works that reach out to help a brother or sister who is in dire need. Such a person may talk about faith, but if there is no walk, there is no real faith.

What use is it to say you have faith if it is not active? One may say the words, but if there are no works to back it up, it is merely empty, religious chatter. A total disconnection exists between the words and the walk.

Verse 17 says, "Even so faith, if it hath not works, is dead, being alone." Such nonworking faith is a dead faith—it is no faith. Now we understand why the Reformers said, "Faith alone saves, but faith that is alone does not save." The last word of this verse, *alone*, is the key. If faith is alone, it means no works are growing out of it. That faith is a dead faith. Whatever confession of faith a person makes, it is a dead confession. Whatever testimony that person gives, it is a dead testimony. There is no living reality to his claim to have faith. Such faith is a non-saving faith.

Falling Short of True Faith

R. C. Sproul again elaborates on this in *The Reformation Study Bible*: "When James says that faith without works is dead, he is describing a faith that knows the gospel." Dr. Sproul says that, first, the facts are in the mind, and second, such a person "even agrees with it." "There is an inward persuasion of its veracity," Sproul writes, "but it has fallen short of trust in God." As described in James 2:17, there is no activating of the will to commit one's life to Christ. That person has never entrusted his life to the Lord Jesus Christ. There is no crossing the line from darkness to life. There is no entering through the narrow gate. There is no drinking of His blood and eating of His flesh. There is no apprehending of Christ by faith. Sproul writes, "Failure to grow, develop, and bear the fruits of righteousness shows that the free gift of God in Christ has never been received."[1] The person in verse 17 whose faith has no works, who possesses a dead faith, is someone who professes Christ but does not possess Him. It is someone who *says* he or she has faith in the Lord but, in reality, does not. Jesus warned, "Not every one that saith unto me, Lord, Lord, shall enter into the kingdom of heaven; but he that doeth the will of my Father" (Matt. 7:21). The evidence is in the active obedience. There must be doing to back up the confessing. Good fruits must result from good roots.

In James 2:18, James anticipates an imaginary objector and writes: "Yea, a man may say, Thou hast faith, and I have works." This is where the objector's argument ends. Then James retorts brilliantly in the second half of the verse: "Show me thy faith without thy works, and I will show thee my faith by my works." The only way you could ultimately know that your faith is a real, saving faith, James says, is by the objective evidence

---

[1] "Faith and Works," X.

of a truly transformed life, one that produces the fruit of good works. Faith is the root; good works is the fruit. The sinner is not saved by the fruit but by the root. The axiom is true: A good tree will produce good fruit (Matt. 7:17). Every good tree evidences itself with good fruit, and every good tree has a good root—a living faith. James is belaboring the difference between someone who merely says he or she has faith and claims to be a Christian but is not, and another person who claims to be a Christian and, in fact, really is. The real difference is below the surface, whether or not a living faith is in the heart that produces the fruit of good works.

5

Non-Saving Faith

Thou believest that there is one God; thou doest well: the devils also believe, and tremble. But wilt thou know, O vain man, that faith without works is dead?

James 2:19–20

James still anticipates someone who disagrees at this point who says, "All you have to do is just walk the aisle and pray the prayer. All you have to do is just say, 'I believe,' even if there is no outward evidence." What about that person? In verse 19, James says to such a person, "Thou believest that there is one God" and argues that this statement is synonymous with someone's making a good confession of Christian orthodoxy. Deuteronomy 6:4 is the *Shema*: "Hear, O Israel: The LORD our God is one LORD." This was considered the ultimate statement of orthodoxy. Since Israel was surrounded by pagan nations with their many pagan idols, God demanded that their confession be monotheistic: that He alone is God and there is no other. This is the confession that there is only one God and every other god is a sham, an imposter, or an empty idol. There is only one true living God. This basic confession represents a fundamental orthodoxy in the core tenets of the truth.

The Primary Example of Non-saving Faith

In verse 19, James challenges his readers who might be saying, "My beliefs are orthodox. Doesn't that get me into heaven?" James answers abruptly with intentional shock: "Thou doest well: the devils also believe, and tremble." Some of the most orthodox statements in the Bible were made by devils. Consider the theologically correct testimonies that were made by demon-possessed people as the demons spoke: "I know thee who thou art, the Holy One of God" (Mark 1:24). But do you want to argue that the demons are saved? Do you want to say that the devil himself is right with God? This demonstrates that it is entirely possible to be theologically orthodox and lost.

Unquestionably, there are right-believing people with a non-saving faith. They say, "I believe, I believe.

God is one." But the fact is, even the demons agree with this. Hell is orthodox in its theology. The demons cross their doctrinal t's; they dot their theological i's. They have great intelligence, being endowed by their Creator with extraordinary brilliance. The demons believe that God is one, yet they absolutely tremble. The demons have it in the mind, and they have it in the emotions. They know the truth of who Jesus is, and they know the gospel. They even know their own judgment at the end of the age. They are emotionally persuaded of the truth, so much so that they tremble in absolute fear. But they have not exercised their will in submission to the Lord Jesus Christ.

Full Head, Empty Heart

This example is set forth to be a sober warning to untold numbers of people who have a non-saving faith. They know and approve the doctrinal statement. They have been baptized and are members of the church. They are there every time the church doors are open, and they serve. But they have never come to the point where they have repented of their sin, where they have turned away from their sin, where they have confessed their sin to God, where they have acknowledged the guilt of their sin, and where they have called on the name of the Lord to save them. They have never come to the end of themselves that Christ might begin. They have never died to self that they might live for Christ. Their faith is a bogus faith; their confession is a sham confession; their hope is a counterfeit faith. In John 2:23–25, John records that there were people who believed on the Lord Jesus Christ, yet He did not commit Himself to them "because he knew all men . . . for he knew what was in man." Jesus did not believe in their belief.

James asks yet another question that separates the wheat from the tares: "But wilt thou know, O vain man, that faith without works is dead?" (James 2:20). Faith without works is useless for justifying. James is urging that such self-deceived persons should give up their dead testimony. It is the ultimate taking of the Lord's name in vain. He is asking, *Are you willing to cling no longer to your non-saving faith that has no good works?* Faith without works is useless to get you into the kingdom of God. It is useless to connect you to the living God. It does not receive the righteousness that comes from God.

6

Justified by Works or by Faith?

Was not Abraham our father justified by works, when he had offered Isaac his son upon the altar? Seest thou how faith wrought with his works, and by works was faith made perfect? And the scripture was fulfilled which saith, Abraham believed God, and it was imputed unto him for righteousness: and he was called the Friend of God. Ye see then how that by works a man is justified, and not by faith only. Likewise also was not Rahab the harlot justified by works, when she had received the messengers, and had sent them out another way? For as the body without the spirit is dead, so faith without works is dead also.

James 2:21–26

James raises still another question in verse 21: "Was not Abraham our father justified by works when he had offered up Isaac his son upon the altar?" This is a key text, and it initially seems to stand in stark contradiction to what Paul says in Romans 3 and 4. How can we be justified both by faith and by works? How are we to untangle this knot?

Two key observations must be made here. First, this reference to when Abraham offered up Isaac is found in Genesis 22. However, when Paul quoted from the Old Testament—"Abraham believed God, and it was imputed unto him for righteousness"—he referenced Genesis 15, not Genesis 22. This is a critical distinction because Genesis 15:6 is when Abraham exercised saving faith in God and was justified. Genesis 15 is when God transferred His own perfect righteousness into the morally bankrupt account of Abraham. But verse 21 references Genesis 22 and what happened later in his sanctification—to an incident three decades after Abraham had been justified by faith. This is a different kind of justification.

Justified by Works?

In Genesis 22, Abraham was already saved. This justification—"being justified by works"—means that Abraham's faith was being validated as genuine. In

Genesis 22, the faith of Abraham was confirmed as a true, living faith. In verse 21, James references this critical point in Abraham's life when he was called by God to take his son—his only son, Isaac—and climb to the top of Mount Moriah and offer him up to God on the altar. That was a test of the genuineness of his faith, a validation of the authenticity of his faith. Abraham had been justified by faith, but now his faith was being justified by works. His good works were authenticating the validity of his faith—a faith first exercised thirty years earlier. Abraham is not being forensically justified in Genesis 22, nor is he being declared righteous by God here. That legal declaration occurred three decades earlier in Genesis 15. In Genesis 22, Abraham's faith is being justified. That is, his faith is being *validated* as a true, living, saving faith through this test of his obedience.

Tests of faith will occur in the lives of all believers. God will bring all His justified ones to certain trials that serve as crisis points. They are opportunities to demonstrate the genuineness of our faith as justified believers. True faith was exercised at the time of our conversion. A trial is not our point of entrance into the kingdom; it becomes, simply, a confirmation and validation that faith is real.

A Faith That Works

James enlarges his argument in verse 22 when he writes: "Seest thou how faith wrought with his works." That is what real faith is—a faith that works. Real faith is a *living* faith that has legs on it, that sits up and walks and moves out in obedience to God. That is what Abraham had. He had a living faith that worked, that propelled him up the mountain to sacrifice Isaac to God. Verse 22 continues, "And by works was faith made perfect?" Abraham had a faith that works. A faith that does not work is not true faith. The expression "made perfect" means that faith must be brought to greater maturity. It needs to be ripened to greater fullness. This very same word is used earlier in James 1: "My brethren, count it all joy when ye fall into divers temptations; knowing this, that the trying of your faith worketh patience. But let patience have her perfect work, that ye may be perfect and entire, wanting nothing" (vv. 2–4).

This sounds exactly like Abraham offering up Isaac. James is saying that God brings trials into our lives to develop and deepen our faith. The word *perfect* pictures fruit that is brought to maturity or ripeness. So it is with faith. It does not mean that our faith becomes absolutely perfect but that it is growing and developing and maturing through the trials we face.

By the Spirit's grace, as we are stretched and developed by trials in our lives, faith is brought to a place of greater maturity. The testing of faith means that it is being deepened and enlarged as we respond properly. When we make choices to obey God amid fiery trials, this develops and matures our faith. But as long as we are sitting on the sidelines, passively observing others, we suffer spiritual atrophy. The muscles of our faith grow weak. But when we stand up and move out and exercise our spiritual muscles, our faith is being perfected. That is what James is saying in verse 22.

James Teaches *Sola Fide*

In verse 23, James writes: "And the scripture was fulfilled which saith, Abraham believed God, and it was imputed unto him for righteousness." James quotes the passage that Paul quotes in Romans 4:3. This is another indication that Paul and James are not contradicting each other, since they are even appealing to the very same Old Testament Scripture in Genesis 15. They are both teaching justification by faith alone, but James is moving further, going beyond the initial act of justification to the ongoing process of sanctification. James is saying that faith alone saves but faith will be tested in order to give evidence that it is true faith. He is arguing that you cannot merely say you are a Christian without there being the clear evidence of a growing faith that produces good works.

If James were teaching forensic justification by faith and works, he would have just slit his own throat. Why would he quote Genesis 15:6, the supreme proof text for justification by faith, unless he believed it? Instead, he is making the very same point that Paul does in Romans. James is bold to quote this verse. Let us be clear: Verse 23 is referencing Genesis 15 when Abraham was justified by faith, while verses 21 and 22 reference Genesis 22, thirty years later when his faith was justified by works.

Verse 24 wraps up this entire argument. "Ye see then how that by works a man is justified, and not by faith only." We get a little nervous and begin to sweat when we hear this. But James is saying *exactly* what Paul is teaching. In fact, it is the very same thing that Moses wrote and that Abraham experienced in Genesis 15:6. Sinners are justified by faith alone, but true faith will never be alone. It will always have good works following it. Let's put it this way: Good works will never lead anyone into the kingdom of God. But once one is in the kingdom, good works will always follow him every step of the way. Works will never justify someone. But once one is justified by faith, that faith will be accompanied by good works. If not, such a person may *claim* to be in the kingdom but really is not. That is the point James is making.

If the root of justification does not produce fruit, the root is dead. The fruit, then, justifies justification.

Rahab: No Works to Save Her

So, who can be saved? James speaks a word of encouragement on this very point in verse 25. It does not matter how sinful you are or how far away from God you are; if you, by grace, put all your faith in Christ, regardless of your sinful past and present, God will justify you. He will remove your sins apart from good works. This is the glory of the doctrine of justification by faith. Verse 25 reads: "Likewise also was not Rahab the harlot justified by works, when she had received the messengers, and had sent them out another way?"

You recall the story of Rahab, recorded in the book of Joshua, in which her good works accompanied her faith. Once saved, she took a great risk and hid the spies at great danger to her own life. But she was no longer a part of the world. Her good works gave evidence that she had entered into God's kingdom. She was willing to put her neck on the line to hide the two spies in Jericho. This was compelling evidence that she was already justified by faith. Here was the proof that her faith was a *living* faith. Rahab—with great courage and boldness, in the face of great danger to her own life—identified with the two spies and hid them.

When verse 25 reads, "Likewise also was not Rahab the harlot justified by works," it means that Rahab's faith was being justified by works. Rahab was justified by faith, and her faith was justified by works. That is, Rahab's faith was validated or proven to be true by her works. This crisis point occurred when she received the messengers and sent them out another way *after* she was already justified.

Verse 26 concludes, "For as the body without the spirit is dead, so faith without works is dead also." If you merely say that you have faith, yet there are no good works, James says you are a spiritual corpse—there is no spiritual life in you. That is what verse 26 is saying, with the intent to provoke the reader to examine themselves to make certain that their faith is a true, living faith—that the roots of faith produce the fruits of faith.

By Faith Alone That Is Not Alone

John Gerstner helps us wrap up this discussion of how faith and works fit together this way:

We can never say too often justification is by faith alone, but not by faith that is alone. Justification is by a working faith. Let me explain, therefore, once again what the Protestant biblical doctrine of justification by faith alone apart from works means. Justification with God is apart from the merit of works. That does not mean that justification is apart from the existence of works. Christianity teaches justification apart from the merit of works. Easy-believism teaches justification apart from the existence of works. Faith without the existence of works is dead. And so, the impact of what James is saying, why we need the book of James in the New Testament, is so that people who know the truth of the Book of Romans, that we are justified by faith alone, may be challenged that it's more than just an intellectual faith in the head, and that [salvation is] more than just an emotional faith in the feelings. But that it is a true faith, a validous faith whereby one has truly exercised their will and committed their life to Jesus Christ. This is the value of James.[1]

---

[1] John H. Gerstner, "The Nature of Justifying Faith," in *Justification by Faith Alone*, ed. Don Kistler (Morgan, PA: Soli Deo Gloria, 2003), 115.

Are we justified by faith or by works? The answer is that we are justified by faith alone. But it is our works that justify our faith. Good works validate that our faith is a living faith—a true, saving faith.

7

The Root Produces the Fruit

We are now in a position to return to our test cases. Should we accept Mr. Jones or Mr. Smith or, perhaps, both? This is painful, of course, but I am hoping you will agree with me: We can accept neither man.

After talking with the consistory or session, we call Mr. Jones back into the room, and as pastor, you say something like this to him: "Mr. Jones, thank you for coming and for being so honest in what you said to us, but we have to inform you that we don't have liberty to accept you, as it is not clear to us that you are a Christian. We hope to work with you in the future, but it appears that as of this moment you do not understand what it means to be converted. In fact, sir, you speak a very different language than the language of God's people. If we are to be straight with you, friend, we would have to say that it appears that you have the spirit of a Pharisee and a legalist, though you may not realize it. You are imagining that you have some goodness or merit of your own that will commend you to God. You do not realize that even your best righteousnesses are as filthy rags before an all-seeing and holy God."

The sort of teaching Mr. Jones needs to put him right is the teaching of Paul—that man is justified by faith alone without works. Mr. Jones needs to read and prayerfully ponder Romans, Galatians, Ephesians, and Philippians, in which Paul tells us that the righteousness we need is not our own. In Philippians, Paul said how he once had the righteousness of the law as a Jew, and he boasted about his parents, his ancestors, his circumcision, and all his blamelessness, according to the ceremonial law. Then he said he found Christ, and what did he say next? "Yea doubtless, and I count all things but loss for the excellency of the knowledge of Christ Jesus my Lord: for whom I have suffered the loss of all things, and do count them but dung, that I may win Christ, and be found in him, not having mine own righteousness, which is of the law, but that which is through the faith of Christ, the righteousness which is of God by faith" (Phil. 3:8–9). That is what Paul came to understand—that justification is by faith alone.

Tragically, today millions of people like Mr. Jones do not have an inkling of what it means to be justified before God. It is a most terrible spiritual state and condition to be in. The kindest thing you can do is to tell such people that they have no faith, no knowledge of God, and that they are deceiving themselves and are on the broad road to destruction. They do not understand even the basics of the gospel.

What about you, my friend? Do you mirror Mr. Jones? If so, you have something to learn, and I pray God will teach you what you need so desperately to know.

But what about Mr. Smith then? Sadly, there are too many Mr. Smiths around. They remind us of John Bunyan's Mr. Talkative. Their problem is the opposite of Mr. Jones. Mr. Jones is a legalist, and Mr. Smith is an antinomian. He has all the right words but nothing to prove the reality of what he has to say. His tongue talks plenty, but his life has not changed. There is nothing holy about this man. He has talk but nothing more. Mr. Smith needs to read and prayerfully ponder the epistle of James. In fact, James wrote his epistle precisely for the kind of evangelical hypocrite that Mr. Smith sadly represents. James says to such people, "Yea, a man may say, Thou hast faith, and I have works: shew me thy faith without thy works, and I will shew thee my faith by my works" (James 2:18).

Allow us to ask you: Do you see fruit in your life being produced, the fruit of good works flowing from the root of faith? Is there a desire in your heart to live in obedience to God? Do you see a growing, habitual, increasing, practice of righteousness in your life? We are not asking you if you are perfect or if you never sin. None of us meets that standard. But do you see within your heart a desire to follow the Word of God and the Lord Jesus Christ? Are you convicted when you sin? Do you feel genuinely sorry when you sin? Do you sense a decreasing love for the world? Do you find within you an increasing love for the things of God? Do you see in your life an increasing practice of righteousness?

If you answer yes to these questions—even a small yes—then there is certainly a true faith rooted within you that is producing fruit. It is not great faith in God that necessarily saves, but it is faith in a great God that saves. It is the presence of good works that validates your faith. As you see these things, it testifies that your faith is a living faith—a true, saving faith. Your roots of faith are not dead and artificial but alive and genuine.

If, on the other hand, you see a dichotomy in your life—that is, you come to church on Sunday and you hear the Word of God, but you go back out in the world and there is no life change—then that would be cause for great concern. That would be a reason to ask yourself, *Is my faith a true faith? Is it a living faith? Is the root of gracious faith within me?*

Faith alone saves, but saving faith will never be alone. It will always be accompanied by good works, even if they are but a small yet growing reality. If you see these good works, you can know that God is at work in your life, both to will and to work for His good pleasure. You can know that you have eternal life as you see such good works arise from your heart. By grace, you may conclude, *This must surely be a supernatural work of grace within me.* Only God could grow you from spiritual infancy, through childhood and teenage years, to a young man or a young woman in the faith, advancing into the maturity of spiritual adulthood in the Lord. As you see this growth in your life, it brings verification that your faith in Christ is genuine. Faith is a gift of God, and it is not of ourselves. When God gives the gift of faith, it is alive. It will always be alive, and it will give evidence of itself through good works.

Paul and James speak with one voice as they teach justification by faith. They just look at this faith from different perspectives. Paul exposes those who say they are saved because they perform the law's rituals and tells them it is only by faith in Christ that they can be saved. He's burrowing down within us to examine the roots of our justification. James exposes the hypocrite who claims to have faith but whose claim is contradicted by his actions—his fruits are artificial, which, in turn, proves that his roots are artificial. Paul says that faith alone saves, and James adds that saving faith is never alone. Saving faith is a faith that works. If we are true Christians, the root of justification must produce the fruit of justification.

More Books by
Free Grace Press

Brian Borgman, *An Exile's Guide to Walking with God: Meditations on Psalm 119*

Daniel Chamberlin, *A Portrait of God: Stephen Charnock's Discourses upon the Existence and Attributes of God Summarized for the 21st Century*

Ron Crisp and Daniel Chamberlin, *Jesus is Lord: The Mediatorial Reign of Christ*

Michael Haykin, *Giving Glory to the Consubstantial Trinity: An Essay on the Quintessence of the Christian Faith*

Don Johnson, *Victory in Jesus: A Devotional Commentary on the Book of Revelation*

Jeffrey Johnson, *He Died for Me: Limited Atonement and the Universal Gospel*, Revised Edition

Jeffrey Johnson, *The Absurdity of Unbelief: A Worldview Apologetic of the Christian Faith*

Benjamin Keach, *The Glory of a True Church*

Tom Nettles, *The Privilege, Promise, Power, and Peril of Doctrinal Preaching*

Tom Nettles, *Easier for a Camel: Andrew Fuller's View of Man's Absolute Dependence on Grace*

Michael Seewald, *Anticipating God's Rest: Theology and Celebration of the Lord's Day*

Henry Scougal, *A Modern Revision of the Life of God in the Soul of Man*

Jeffery Smith, *Preaching for Conversions*

Kurt Smith, *Piety, Passion, Paradox: The Life and Legacy of Basil Manly, Sr*

Sam Waldron, *The Crux of the Free Offer of the Gospel*

Jeremy Walker, *On the Side of God: The Life and Labors of Andrew Fuller*

Thomas Wilcox, *A Choice Drop of Honey from the Rock of Christ*

Jerome Zanchius, *Absolute Predestination*, A Modern Reprint